S

Gospel (

Smallwords

Sharon Morris

Gospel Oak

ENITHARMON PRESS

First published in 2012
by Enitharmon Press
26B Caversham Road
London NW5 2DU

www.enitharmon.co.uk

Distributed in the UK by
Central Books
99 Wallis Road
London E9 5LN

ISBN: 978-1-907587-23-8

British Library Cataloguing-in-Publication Data.
A catalogue record for this book is available
from the British Library.

Designed in Albertina by Libanus Press
and printed in England by
Antony Rowe Ltd

CONTENTS

But to be alone is to be lost
Altho the tree, the roots
Are there

It is an oak: the word
Terrifying spoken to the oak —
George Oppen

1

... somehow we know by instinct that outsize buildings
cast the shadow of their own destruction before them,
and are designed from the first
with an eye to their later existence as ruins.
W. G. Sebald

FALL

feallan, fallanan, -phol –

not a question of morality,

choice or control,

that incendiary burn out of summer,

flames of maple and red pin oak,

sycamore burnt orange;

horse chestnut the first to wither, not

through drought or cold

but eaten by moths;

brown leather leaves of English oak

cleave spare to the mast of winter;

the City viewed from Hampstead Heath

as though incommensurate.

Mouldering leaves.
Rotting wood. Decay. Change
in the air.

Acorns, conkers, sweet chestnuts, beech and hazelnuts fall,

accumulate the sweet mast
of history,
when pigs and boars rooted for pannage;

seeds split open according to the laws of matter,

utterly familiar

and yet
the specifics
as unpredictable

as the way we fall in love
or into hell –

the forgotten,
the fallen.

PARLIAMENT HILL

The kind of London day, drear,
that could sap all will;
no wind for flying kites, the city,
like expectation itself,
subjugated
under low grey cloud.

This hill, named Traitors' Hill,
where Roundheads rallied
against Cavaliers;
Parliamentarians, Diggers
and Levellers opposing
the king's divine right to rule.

Eleven years without parliament,
seven years without a king:
a failed English revolution?
class struggle? progress
towards democracy?
or a British civil war?

Site of druidic disputation
under God's eye,
then a Saxon moot, today
the white Stone of Free Speech
is smeared red,
its writing unintelligible.

Follow me – upstream
in the course of this
dried riverbed,

river once as wide and deep
as the Ganges
flowing from the west,
depositing banks
of golden sand from Devon, glittering
with eyes of amber;
Bagshot sand layered with seams of flint
from Salisbury Plain;

fine silt settled from the colloid of mud,
claygate beds,
unstable sand and clay;
water rich in iron springing
from the spring line,
at the meeting point
of impervious
thin layers of pipe clay;

clods of blue London clay,
the bricks of London stock,
sticking to our boots,
legacy of warm swamps
when hippos wallowed
in Trafalgar Square,
crocodiles in Islington;

short worn grass over chalk,
friable as the sea shells
of the ever present sea;

our feet suddenly
hitting solid ground,
the Devonian bedrock hefted
onto the surface,
scoured and scraped by ice;

and then that tipping point,
the full spate
of debris-littered
glacial melt.

ROSIN

There are days when I can't get
up until midday, e-mail

unopened, mobile switched
off, no radio or TV, no news,

when I remain beneath
the wire, just able to haul myself

over the Heath, obdurate
as an old horse, blinkered head

hung down in refusal; days
when rolling the resin of pine

between my finger and thumb
brings the scent of a violin

and too much reality.

DROVERS' ROADS

From here, the path resembles
a road in a vast landscape
of wilderness,

except the father with a child
on his shoulders
changes the scale –

I am holding my hands
in front of my face, measuring,
framing. Small streams

lurch and burn their sharp-lit
byways, arteries of London
swollen with rain;

distant swish of tyres
at Spaniards Inn, the toll house
for the drovers' roads

stamped by the hooves of cattle,
leather-soled pigs,
tarred feet of ducks and geese;

ten thousand animals each day
prodded by the drover's goad
from Wales and the north

to Smithfield; a horned contusion
of bulls and cows, tails tied;
sheep squeezed into hurdles

tight as figs in a drum
and as silent; deafening, pigs
shrieking, cattle bellowing,

oxen roaring, dogs howling,
men shouting and cursing,
the dull blow of sticks

never-ending:
breath of animals,
breath of fear, white in the carnal

cold air of the slaughter houses
and gut-scraperies;
acres of wool, roods of pigskin,

reeking with blood and dung;
stomach-churning,
the stench of the triperies

CONSTABLE'S VIEW

Branch Hill Pond,
1820, 1825,
1830, his gaze
cast wide over Middlesex
to Harrow-on-the-Hill,
a thick impasto
of scarified green, burnt umber,
ochre, glowing
on a black-primed ground,
flecks of Chinese white catching
specular reflections,
the kind of beauty
that comes with light
as an assertion of will
in a time of apathy
and futility.

Under this vast sky
there is a curious lack
of foreground –
an abysmal gap
between us,
the onlookers,
and in the middle distance,
a horse and cart, boy, cows
and even more curiously,
given Constable's adage
the great vice of the present day
is bravura, an attempt
to do something beyond the truth,
an imaginary
windmill.

Paddington Basin: Carmine, Monsoon, Battleship, Cucumber.
Battersea's vision of a Green Bird.

Constant revolutionising of production,

City of London: Walkie Talkie/Pint, Helter Skelter/Pinnacle,
Heron Tower, Cheesegrater, Tower 42, Gherkin.

uninterrupted disturbance of all social conditions,

Shadowing St Paul's: the Stealth Bomber, Vortex,
Rothschild's Sky Pavilion, groundscraper engine block for UBS.

everlasting uncertainty and agitation . . .

South of the river: Shard, Quill, Strata, Razor/Isengard,
Boomerang, Doon Street Tower.

All fixed, fast-frozen relations . . . are swept away . . .

Isle of Dogs: Canary Wharf, Tower 42, Riverside South,
One Canada Square, FSA, the Pride.

All that is solid melts into air, all that is holy is profaned . . .

DECIDUOUS

decidere – to fall down, to fall off

Like antlers,
fish scales,
skin discarded every day,
hair that falls out every six years,
muscles wasted without use,
skeleton replaced every twelve years,
breath exchanged forty times per minute,
blood pulsed sixty beats per second,
continual loss and renewal of cells,
self
and the assiduous mind forced
to change
with the wind
and season

as we try through these acts of abscission
to rid ourselves of guilt,
fear,
regret,
even joy,
secret pleasures,
wanting redress.

After the blaze of colour
the fall is always lachrymose.

LAPSUS

Everywhere, deadwood –
branches ripped from swaying trees,
twigs scattered
as though from the nests of crows
abandoned
at the first sign of disaster.
A slip of clay welters towards the ponds,
water brims
over the levee
and floods towards Oak Village.

Eerie, this sulphurous light
and the dark underbelly of cloud.
Lapsus, a slip of the tongue,
mind, memory.
The ash has collapsed
onto its lower branches
like a sick horse
too heavy to rise on its own.
Children
ride on its back.

HARVEST

It has come to fruition.
Crab apples and wild apple trees christened
with small tart apples;
hedgerows shiny with hedge currants,
blackberries oozing black juice,
hips and haws rich with vitamin C,
bitter sloes and checkers left to blet in the frost;
the woodland floor scattered with nuts
that roll under our feet like ball bearings –
we are the new gleaners, foragers, rooting like wild boar,
squirrels hoarding madly
against darkness.

A cedar of Lebanon gives shelter
to Constable's grave;
the graveyard of St John-at-Hampstead
dominated by the spire he painted so often,
its roseate window casting
a wreath of flowers and fruits
onto the stone floor.

HALLOWE'EN

Between the fall of the world
and the high pitch
of things to come,

when the veil between us
is thin we remember them,
the spoken for.

Burn logs of oak and yew
in the bonfires of Celtic New Year,
Samhain,

make hallow our bones –
hollow as the bones of birds
and prepare for flight.

A RING, A RING O' ROSES

A rash of red bites
        from fleas carried
on the backs of rats, living
        in the sewers
of London; rivers red
        with fly-blown meat
and rotting carcasses,
        the bubonic Fleet
open to the air, piss
        and shit oozing
down the walls:

        we are the plagued,
locked in our houses
        by doctors clothed
in vinegar-soaked
        robes, long-beaked
masks filled with
        bergamot oil,
bearing pouches
        of sweet-scented
herbs.
        Burn us –

Art is not a mirror

        art is a hammer:

don't you hear

        we're at war?

don't we fear

        you're at war?

don't you believe

        we're at war?

don't we grieve

        you're at war?

aren't you flooded

        by war?

aren't you bloodied

        in war?

aren't we maimed

        by war?

aren't we to blame

        you're at war?

don't you drown

        in war?

don't we own

        this war?

haven't we earned

        this war?

aren't you burned

        by war?

don't you dream

        we're at war?

aren't you damned

        we're at war?

aren't we drummers

        of war?

Art, it is said, is not a mirror, but a hammer: it does not reflect, it shapes. But at present even the handling of a hammer is taught with the help of a mirror…

art is a hammer.

you're at war?

we're at war?

you're at war?

we're at war

by war?

in war?

by war?

we're at war?

in war?

this war?

this war?

by war?

you're at war

you're at war?

of war?

Art is not a mirror

don't we hear

don't you fear

don't we believe

don't you grieve

aren't we flooded

aren't we bloodied

aren't you maimed

aren't you to blame

don't we drown

don't you own

haven't you earned

aren't we burned

don't we dream

aren't we damned

aren't you drummers

*If one cannot get along without a mirror, even
in shaving oneself, how can one reconstruct
oneself or one's life, without seeing oneself in
the 'mirror' of literature?*

Acheron of pain and grief, the first
                    lengthy sting of conscience;

Phlegathon, a stream of fire,
                    circling the earth,
                        red with blood of the tortured;

Styx, the sewer of hatred,
                    winding around hell
                        that is our defence
                                against feelings,
                        against truth;

                    locked
in the frozen tears
                    of the Cocytus, wailing
                        for the unburied dead –

                                all that is deferred,
                    displaced,
dismissed and disavowed;

                    seek neither the oblivion
                of the Lethe,
                    wiping out all our memories,

        nor the Eunoe, restoring only the good,

                    look instead for the small cool stream
                that springs directly

                    from the side of the hill.

CRYING THE NECK

'The neck! The neck! The neck!'
Grasp the last sheaf
of living crop,
cut with scythe and sickle,
tie at the waist,
tie at the neck,
and cry a long lament of relief.

'Murder! Murder! Murder!'
Carry it inside
and hang over the hearth;
harvest moon red,
casting shadows
of ritual, atavistic,
over the city stubble.

GREEN MASK

Last night, eyes wide
open, I saw
a leafless branch
on my bedroom wall:
'rip out the dead wood'
a voice whispered.

That green foliate mask,
my skin, shed
like a snake's, I am sinking
into the earth,
slow peristalsis of winter
swallowing.

It is time to bring in
the tender plants,
mulch with straw
and dry leaves,
cover roots with bark
and black plastic.

2

When the times darken
will there be singing even then?
There will be singing even then
of how the times darken.
Bertolt Brecht

THE DEPOSITORY OF WINTER

Obliterating all difference
that last Ice Age
20,000 years ago,

shrinking the sea,
sinking the land,

then the great thaw,
splitting white
into the full spectrum of colour,
the diversity of things,

a northward drift
of the tree-line,
at first coniferous
then deciduous,
small wild flowers in the tundra,

brown bear and caribou
followed by deer,

boar by wild pig,
the migration of Mesolithic people
walking from Europe

before the island flood,
the land still rising, tilting,
but more slowly than the sea –

my dream recurs,
a trough in the ocean,
a depression in the water.

TREES IN WINTER

Trees –
they know the recess
of winter, how
to retreat,
continue bereft of leaves
without grief,
as though practising
the acts of dying;
branches
braced
motionless,
seemingly supported
by freezing air,
frame the view
to the city;
fine adventitious roots
like the repressed,
multiply,
stretching way out beyond
the drip-line;
taproots strike
veridical
into the hiemal earth,
that deep
blue lake:
not yet the cessation
of things.

IN MEMORIAM

Tense this city, wreathed
in grey, heavy as lead;

staid cranes moored
at Canary Wharf

like the tall ships that sailed
from West India docks,

a trade of guns and cloth
in exchange for white gold,

sugar, rum, molasses;
built on the backs of slaves

city towers of glass and steel
gleam dull in the half-light,

illusory in their tall grief.

NO PLACE AT ALL

The North London Line
used to be called the Silver Link,
a more appropriate name
for this prelapsarian train idling
towards Richmond
past Parliament Hill –
the green fields, lido, running track and allotments,
neat plots of brassicas, giant onions and leeks,
dwarf-stock fruit trees,

except at night, when you can't sleep,
you can hear the weight of the heaviest rolling-stock,
lead-lined concrete trucks of nuclear waste
on its way to Sellafield.

FALLING DEGREES

Starlings. A crop of odd
fruit. Suddenly gone.

Fox on the wall.
Tracks not melting.

Snow clouds beyond the city
I mistake for hills.

Uneasy, standing
under the frosted pine.

THE DEVIL IN THE DETAIL

A Christmas card,
a painting by Breughel,
this one day of snow, silencing
the city, halts the buses and underground
first time since the blitz; the Heath a fairground
helter-skelter of slides on plastic trays and stolen bin lids,
Russian-style sleighs and hi-tech snowboards, treacherous ski
slopes to iced ponds where cartoon ducks skid to a halt;
a rush and shriek of laughter, children pelt each other
with snow, rolling giant globes of snow gathering
dirt like terminal moraine; carving snowmen
and snow women, all curvature, breasts,
hair of twigs, and fine, fine fingers
of willow –
these are glyphs
of the Frost Fairs,
when horse and carriages
crossed the frozen river, fish
suspended in ice, bear and bull-baiting,
stalls for coffee, ale and wine, butchers and bakers,
barbers, prostitutes, hawkers and costermongers, oysters
slipping down the gullet, hunting fox on the *white path* from Whitehall
to London Bridge; then, the sudden thaw shoving those standing on ice-floes
into the smashed blocks of ice, flooding crazily downstream,
wrecked ships, flotsam, jetsam and thousands of dead fish
spewing out of its mouth, the Thames at Gravesend,
and flushed into the North Sea.

MIDWINTER SOLSTICE

When the sun hangs still
over London,

when the sun hangs low
on the horizon,

then the king of oak
kills the king of holly;

mummers, rhymers, soulers,
dumb and ludic play

the green knight slaying evil,
wassail and burn the Yule log

before the lengthening day,
return of the liminal

twilight and the wash
of blue before dawn.

THE MEN'S POND

Beside the boathouse a small boat is locked in ice.

A goose walks with a slow gait into mist that rimes
        the opposing bank.

A man dives into the single patch of open water.

On the levee we stand and wait one thought in mind.

In Amsterdam a friend skating on the canal falls
        and cracks his shoulder. Coeval.

KAIROS

Not floating and not,
as in my dream,
a small bare tree
just above the ocean
waves, weeping,

a beech tree
stands in the pond
solid; the flat plane
of ice cutting
its first boughs –

past and future
held timeless,
we are waiting for
this moment
to force through.

GREENMANS

the town is simply disguised countryside

See him slip on horseback
through the streets of London!
His skin green, his face
a mask of green leaves,
his hair and beard long
to his elbows, green.
His clothes green, embroidered
with butterflies and birds.
Green jewels glitter.
His horse clad in green
hung with green tassels.
Horse and rider
threaded iridescent gold.
He holds in one hand
a branch of holly
and in the other an axe
forged from green steel.
He is the Green Knight.
His green lips command
                behead him!

COMMON LAND

You can tell the age of a hedgerow
by its constituency of bush and tree –
hagas of hawthorn, blackthorn, quickthorn,
hazel, hornbeam, field maple;
willow, lashed to pales
marking the bounds of feudal estates, Hampstead
and Tottenhall,
dividing sunny demesne from common land –
wasteland, heath, bog, scrub, forest,
the glints of villeins and serfs and their common rights:
common of pasture,
              grazing for their stint of goats, sheep and pigs;
common of estovers,
              furze, gorse and whill for bedding and fuel,
              fallen wood for tools;
common of turbary,
              peat for roofing and fire;
common of piscary,
              pike and carp;
nothing for the slaves
              deemed already dead.

These ancient oaks of Parliament Hill
legacy to the three-field system
and the three-fold division of class –
oratores, who pleaded with God and dispensed absolution;
bellatores, the nobility, knights and warriors who defended the land;
laboratores, ploughmen and cattlemen, whose labour supported everything;
and the non-classified craftsmen of the guilds, merchants,
Jews, Gypsies, outlaws, slaves, women.

SANDY HEATH

Great oaks perch on hillocks,
their roots left hanging,
sacrificed for sand –
a scarred wasteland of extraction,
shapeless heaps of waste,
hideous potholes dug by hand
fifteen metres deep
…
big enough to bury the corpses of a nation
for half a century
at the ordinary rate of mortality . . .
Illustrated London News, 1871.

Bagshot sand, washed here
after the last Ice Age –
sand for building houses, roads,
the Midland railway
to St Pancras;
sandbags for damping bombs
and damming the Thames.

Now, a silent wedge of heathland
between two roads,
seeded with apples gone wild,
the only place on the Heath
I've heard a sparrowhawk shriek,
and where I feel the dark
even in the sun.

TERRIBLE STEED

You, hanging
on the tree of the world,
linking
hell to sky,

where are the wolves and eagles to warn of fire?

Cut off your ear
so that you may hear
the growth of forest, leaf and flower,
rustling small creatures,
the swan drinking.

Take an axe to the oak
to find its root, *deru, doru,*
dru –
meaning truth.

Send out your soul on horseback
to those places torn by war.

Bear a poultice of mud
to heal our wounds,
inflicted
by those monstrous acts
only the hawk sees.

CROWS

A burn of crows,
tremor of crows,
terror of crows,
murder of crows:

black flags untethered from a grey sky,
holes into nothingness,
stumps of night
hunched over a corpse;

carrion crows
corvus corone corone
cleaning the putrefying dead;

making hooks, knives and tools from leaves and grass,
storing thousands of seeds and remembering each location;
crows who learn from each other
and mimic us.

LEG O' MUTTON POND

I am waiting for the unthought known
to surface as though an extinct fish

from the depths of Leg o' Mutton Pond,
where archaeologists found post-holes

of a Mesolithic camp, a midden of flints,
scrapers, microburins, microliths,

chipped and faceted into knives and arrows,
pebbles, porcelain-crackled in fire –

oh, to have the vision of this heron
watching the water drain into the river Brent.

GALANTHUS NIVALIS

Out of this grime, dirty rags of snow
and treacherous black ice,

like a bell calling us, the longing,
to Candlemas,

this white flower, image of fragility hung
on a slender pedicel,

translucent and resilient as porcelain,
driven out of the earth

by white-tipped leaves hard as steel,
returned from the corm

insistent and perennial,
is hammered

into a white light searing its concentration
pure.

3

Still the walls do not fall,
I do not know why . . .
                    H. D.

SPRING

It is in virtue of unity that beings are beings ...
What could exist at all except as one thing?

Sprengh –

    springing time –

        sprhayati (desire) –

           a rapid jolt

the holt of ash

    green florets   burst

      from black ashen buds.

      This year before the oak

a phenology of hope   spurt of leaf from dirt

    crumpled flowers   slit out of bare bark

that drive to exist deep-   throated hum of spring

    he continuum   made denumerate

        each

  and every   thing

      accidental

as the erratic flight of a butterfly shunted

    out of the crowd

(this year so many butterflies).

A random mutation   tychism becoming habit

    emergence of complexity

      our meaning

this day threaded with sun   first lovers on the bench.

    How can we discriminate?

    each hue and shade –

      green

divisible
and made infinite
(comfort in this act of counting)

yet fathomless
as the spring's source
underground

a coil of bird shit on the warm stone
of Bird Bridge

the stream's vital surface
shattered into stars.

Personhood
a constellation seen from our own point of view

I am your   eyes, ears, mouth   and no mind.

WHAT CANNOT BE FORGOTTEN

Before maps –
rivers and streams, holy wells, bridges,
stiles, stones and great trees
marked the edge of our world;
village rights of birth and death
beaten into the body.

An annual procession walked
the bounds of Gospel Oak
down the watershed of west meadow,
Saxon ditch and river Fleet
to Haverstock Hill;
boys were whipped with willow
until they cried, bumped on stones
and dunked in water.

Stopped under the Gospel oak
for the blessing of crops,
women holding knots of wild flowers.

HEATH EXTENSION

Aspen, Anglo-Saxon for *Populus tremula*,
shivers, as if with joy
                    and expectation,
in this slender breeze
that whispers across the flat plain
south of Hampstead Garden Suburb,
Lutyens' conical spire,
St Jude-on-the-Hill, piercing the sky,
a wide yawning arc over Wylde's farmland,
immense as the vision
of an egalitarian world;
                    or shakes
with the tremens of fear, the way
an animal deals with trauma,
as though the ACAC guns of World War II
continue to reverberate
through the mute ponds, the Seven Sisters
bordered with forget-me-nots,
a flash of kingfisher once in a blue moon.

THE SUBJECT

There is the world –
it passes through me as a cloud of information,
avatars of memories and feelings
like flies over a pond glinting sharp flecks of metal,
then stills.

I find you like an animal, choleric, disgruntled, fretful
inside me
and I attach myself to you
like a magpie standing on the back of a wild pig.

LANDBOARDER

Yellow ripstop nylon splits
from the blue weft of sky
inscribing a hypnotic
curlicue script
like smoke from the chain of beacons
lit along the south coast
and relayed inland
to warn of invasion –
the Spanish Armada
razed at sea
by the English hellburners,
unmanned ships filled with gunpowder.

Tethered to the commemorative flagpole
at Jack Straw's Castle,
the red cross of England flutters
and drops; the man still attached
to his power kite.

MAY DAY

They danced around the maypole,
plaited coloured ribbons, laughing,

girls washing their faces with dew,
hoping to be crowned May queen,

hiding under the wicker *'oss,*
boys reeling and sweating, dressed

in white linen with blood-red sashes,
chasing through hedgerows

of hawthorn and blackthorn, afroth
with white flowers, spinning and

miming the *'oss* 'til they all fell down;
then they burned the wicker man.

Light again the Beltane fires on
the hills of London, *bealltainn, bhel,*

let the flames flicker in the city glass:
this is the time to watch the May,

this is the time to call for help,
this is the time to call for action,

here we go round the Cornhill pole,
here we go round the merry-go-round,

this is the time to raise the alarm,
this is the time to raise the *'oss,*

mayday, m'aider, seelonce.

LIVING MY LIFE BACKWARDS

There were days
when I would sit on a bus

to the end of the line –
I was lost

and it was something to do,
it cost only a single fare

starting in Victoria on the 29
ending up at Wood Green:

I wanted wood,
I wanted green.

WANTING GREEN

Green   green   man
               he will   strangle me

finger buds   of snowdrop
                 crocus, bluebell   wild iris

                                          lily –

                 disgorged leaves
spewing from his

                 nose,   ears   eyes
                                     open mouth

           stem   and stalk   shooting
                 from marled earth

                 splitting the bulb

                 that is his skull.

          Gro   *groh*   unstoppable

                 growing knotted tendrils

                 chthonic snakes of nightmare –

                 high scent of sweet May

                 drenched in pure sun.

THE LONDON PLANE

I can't breathe –
thick white motes of pollen
shed by London planes
stick in my throat,
their hairs, abrasive.
Outside the hospital they stand
attached to intravenous drips:
my pulse quickens
in that place of madness,
where everything
is like everything else,
each part inseparable from its whole
and I could step off the planet
in our descent
entropic,
into that inert
gospel sea of dark velvet.
I am searching for friends
in the long-fallow system, fields
at rest
in the seasonal flow
of things, I believe
inviolable.

LADY DAY

Equal day
and night

the earth tilts
to the sun,

sun streaming
down her face,

equal light
and shade, I

want to hide
my face in

her shadow,
the surge of

spring tides
pulling

the chora
from my heart.

HOSPITAL

In the hospital a woman is dying:
in the hospital a woman is born:
the Thames coils grey, shiny,
around the black tower of Guy's.
Ice plasma shoots through my arm.
I stand on the edge of a cliff. *Don't
jump!* and I turn, take the stairs
down to the medicine man who
holds the turtle of the world; I fall
on the floor as if drunk. A nurse
takes my wrists, counts one, two,
three, four and breathe –
but my nostrils fill with sand,
my body turns to stone; living
my life backwards in an endless
dying, I wait for your return,
listening to her coughing and
the rabbi's whispered voice,
until all sound is one rhythm
and the river a river of light.

WATER GLASS

New blood rushes through me
opening each vein and artery,
colder than my blood, branching
from my arm, successive; I wait
for the sharp needles to strike
my heart and thorn at my lips.
I am broken down as though
this plasma is water glass, silicate
used for preserving eggs and
hardening artificial stone. Shards
of glass under my fingernails fall
away, revealing fine new skin.

Next year I will listen to the sap
rise from the root, rustling to each
branch, to the leaves and finally
the bowers of flowers and fruit.

OAK APPLE DAY

Take an iron pot, pestle and mortar,
1lb of oak marble galls, bruise
then steep in a gallon of water,
add iron sulphate and gum arabic,
macerate for a day until black
and in the air, blacken:

take inspiration from the gall
in this ink and let yourself speak;
write new laws and beware
of the personhood of corporations;
remember *Strength Is Unity*
and shake out the oak.

RIVERS UNDERGROUND

I saw the electric streams of current like liquid
metal, linking the boroughs and monuments of London,
ley lines, mirrors of rivers underground, rinsing –

*

Walbrook tunnelling under Shoreditch and boring, violent,
under the Bank of England, its vaults of gold,
the Temple of Mithras and site of Roman skulls.

From Shepherd's Well the Tyburn shapes the contours
of Marylebone Lane to Grosvenor and Berkeley Squares,
Buckingham Palace; Tyburn brook to the gallows.

Two-headed Fleet, river of wells, St Chad's,
Black Mary's; Fleet-ditch of scum and filth scoured
by toshers; Wren's vision of a new Venice.

Kilburn's Westbourne, its legacy in street names, Westbourne
Terrace, Eastbourne Mews, Milborne Grove;
dammed for the Serpentine Lake to beautify the park.

Frequented by Roman galleys buried in mud,
sailed by Canute and Elizabeth I, visiting
Walter Raleigh, the Effra remains open to the air.

Black Ditch, *Blake broke,* rising at Stepney flumes
into the Thames, marked on the map only as a sewer,
a storm drain of London, sentinel against the flood.

*

I heard the popping in my ear of truth and its attunement.
I saw my life like light.
I felt that moment change falling into the tryst of dream.

INDWELLING

A woman holds the head of a man
in her lap, brother, husband,
friend or lover,
asleep on a bench

and I long to hold the shape of a nest
in my hands.

Someone, with nowhere else to sleep,
has built a shelter
from fallen branches

in this glade of bluebells, so blue,
it seems infinite.

In this choiring, the soul looks upon the wellspring of Life – each scent of thorn separate, discriminate – froth of white flowers – hawthorn/quickthorn/whitethorn/blackthorn, May – Bend down – to the wash of blue, bluebell, Spanish/English (paler, more scented, pre-figuring death) – to the lily, wood anemone, lesser/greater celandine, pink purslane, campion, violet/dog-violet, primrose/butter-rose (pink-eyed/thrum-eyed), cuckoopint/arum/lord and lady/Adam and Eve/bobbin/wake Robbin (spathe sheathed around spadix) – to the honey-sweet yellow anther, the pungent leaf of/stalk of ramson/wild garlic – the damp earth warm, well-lit before the canopy of leaf, sun after rain each twig and branch glassy – Look up through the cut buds/catkins, to new leaves – each blade velvet-bloom/shiny, serrated/ smooth, holly/ilex – oval/boat/lobed – alder, beech, wild service, sycamore, maple, lime, London plane – pure//hybrid oak, common/ uncommon, pedunculate/sessile, English/durmast, Turkey, American red, cork//Lucombe – squint through the screen of set/array – compound leaflets alternate/paired opposing – mountain ash, false acacia/common ash – palmate chestnut horse/sweet, framing the light, dappling the sun – overlapping hands concealing blue, white/ grey scudding clouds – Skying a mackerel sky, what individuates the haecceity of cloud? – pileus, pannus, velum, incus, mamma, virga, tuba, fumulus — be dazzled by the effects of light in air – halo, mock sun/sun-dog/parhelion, arc, corona, iris, glory – Listen to the volary, aggregation, roost, mess, leach, drove, aerie, rout, flew of birds – How many notes, mother? – lowing/bellowing of bullfinches, chime/ family/herd of wrens, cloud/keg/merl of blackbirds, hermitage/muta-tion/rash of thrushes – calls of alarm/defence/attraction/mating/birth – contusion/mischief/ tiding/charm/tribe/murder of magpies – a *cri de coeur* – call and answer/hunger – chatter/clutter/hosting/murmura-tion/ cloud/filth/ scourge/congregation of starlings – too numerous to count, wing-beats imperceptible – charm/chirm/chirp of goldfinches, red-faced, wresting seeds from pine cones – jays/parakeets escaped from a circus – one pair of kestrels soaring, *kee kee, kee kee, kee kee, kee* – descant – veridical to that vernal sky – Hum of traffic in the distance – a woman strolls by learning a score by heart.

4

I Can Walk Through the World
as Music
Philip Corner

TO THE SOURCE

Sourse,

sourdre, to rise,

surgere-

walk with me:

follow the green

through the dry oaten grass,

the green of nettles, thistles, clover, sorrel,

the dampness

where condensation rolls

over the dip and swell

of the land,

rinsing through Bagshot sand and layers of flint,

funnelled into the welt

of chalybeate,

leaching horizontally over thin clay beds

to spring from the navel

as that *wyllspring*:

run-off tethered into rills and rivulets

rivus,

reiwol,

rei-,

trickling

through the puddled ponds

of *Caen-wood,*

sinking as that deep surge

cold as hell,

into the lake of guilt,

pulling

under Parliament Hill,

the eastern stream

straumaz, stram,

strom, stroom, sreu-

willing its confluence
with the western branch
hulled from the Vale of Health,

this tranquil pond
so still
and painful,

a perfect circle of water-lilies,
imperceptible,
its drift   idling

through the dense underlay
of horsetail, reed, bulrush and sphagnum moss,

the ooze picking up momentum
into the hollow stream,

Oldbourne, Holburna, Holbourne,
whittling south east,

becoming the river Fleet,
fleotan, fleot, fl_ot,
flod,

at Anglers Lane,
Caen-ditch Town,
Ken-ditch town,

anchor of the Thames
at its tidal reach.

THE REPETITIOUS HOWLS OF HISTORY

I want to know
what made them as miserable as rain,

the *Dismal Hounds* of Fenton House,
this pair of eighteenth-century porcelain dogs;

I want to hear
what they heard

above the music of harpsichords and virginals,
clavichords, spinets and square pianos.

A WEEK OF TERROR

A time of war:
Spain, France, the war of American Independence.

A time of darkness:
poverty, squalor, inflation, slavery, unemployment,
hatred of popery,
fear of an absolute monarchy.

A week of terror:
king mob, men and women of all races, spilling
through the streets of London,
aflame with gin;
pulling down prison gates;
beating at the doors of the Bank of England,
Downing Street and the Palace;
attacking Catholics, Lords, and the voting classes;
setting ablaze Lord Mansfield's house,
pursued up Millfield Lane by troops ordered to kill.

A week of fire:
cities of fire, cities of rage, London, Bath, Bristol;
the Gordon Riots, 1780.

LONDON'S FIRST SOUVENIR

The Hollow Elme of Hampstead,
an engraving by Wenceslaus Hollar
dated 1653,
shows the great elm where puritans
gathered to hear the Hot Gospellers;
forty-two steps inside its bole
led to an octagonal platform
offering a view to Harrow, Acton
and the Thames, ships and barges
sailing to Hampton Court.

One of those lofty elms, an English
elm, so beloved by Constable;
his tight focus on the parched-
earth fissures of bark,
his gaze scrutinising how
each tree is rooted in the earth.
A world of vast canopy
and elmy shade, landscape
overlaid with lengthening shadows
as though foreshadowing death –
leaves torched red, bark
etched by elm beetle,
wood revealed white as bone.

Elmwood, resistant to water,
used for pipes and boats;
breathing wood; coffinwood.
Ten million felled in three years,
one in a hundred thousand immune.
We are waiting for their return.

THE CREATION – plasterers
CREATION OF THE WORLD – drapers, hosiers
CREATION OF ADAM AND EVE – cardmakers, fullers
THE FALL OF MAN – coopers, barrelmakers
THE EXPULSION – armourers
CAIN AND ABEL – glovers
FALL OF LUCIFER – bakers, tanners
NOAH AND THE FLOOD – shipwrights, fishers, mariners
ABRAHAM AND ISAAC – parchmentmakers, bookbinders
ANNUNCIATION – spicers
THE NATIVITY – wheelrights, slaters, tylers, daubers, thatchers
SHEPHERDS – chandlers, embroiderers
HEROD – vintners
THE THREE KINGS – mercers, spicers
PURIFICATION – hatmakers, masons, labourers
SLAUGHTER OF THE INNOCENTS – girdlers, nailers
CHRIST IN THE TEMPLE – spurriers, lorrimers
BAPTISM – barbers
TEMPTATION – smiths
WOMAN TAKEN INTO ADULTERY – butchers, capmakers
RISING OF LAZARUS – glovers, parchment-makers
COMING OF CHRIST INTO JERUSALEM – skinners
CONSPIRACY – cutlers
THE LAST SUPPER – baxters
AGONY IN THE GARDEN – cordwainers
CRUCIFIXION – shearmen, pinners, ironmongers, ropers
DEATH OF CHRIST – butchers
HARROWING OF HELL – cooks, tapsters, ostlers, innkeepers
THE RESURRECTION – winedrawers
ASCENSION – tailors
PENTECOST – potters
DOUBT OF THOMAS – scriveners
ANTICHRIST – hewsters, bellfounders
THE LAST JUDGEMENT – weavers, walkers, mercers

SUMMER

Green laid over my face
becomes me,
coddled leaf of nettle, flower
of cowslip and ragwort,
grass grows
from my scalp

and I am one
with the mask of summer,
sumor, sumur,
sem, sama,

this season
of butterflies,
small copper,
yellow brimstone,
speckled wood
indiscernible
from bark,

the way you and I mimic and
become each other,
camouflage
the heart.

SUMMER PICNIC

Hampstead is the place to ruralize
On a summer's day.

Hand, foot, top of a head, sun umbrella
just visible above the dry flattened grass,
plastic chairs, hammocks slung
between Scots pine,
numerous carrier bags, ice-cooler, hamper,
occasionally a hubble-bubble,
beat-box, drummer, guitar players, string quartet
with double bass,
a thin line of smoke from an illicit barbecue
strikes into blue
above the city furnace, heat-haze
in the high 30s,
pollution index in the red.
Here we lie indolent
as the golden coy carp floating
alongside the sham bridge,
where long-horned cattle gracing the fields
of Kenwood's *ferme ornée*
were milked in Dido's dairy,
and deer in the deer park lay in the shade.
Families idle their weekends,
taking a stroll in the manner of the leisured classes
along avenues of fir and lime,
children laughing
where Karl Marx played horse and hussars
with his children, picnicked
on roast veal and drank beer
at Jack Straw's Castle,
the location of the gibbet elm.
This late afternoon, bats' flight the only speed,
I am reading Keats's 'Ode on Indolence'
for its radical view of life.

EVERYDAY

Bruce passes by with his daughter's Rhodesian ridgeback.

No contrails the sky an absolute volcanic blue sparkles.

Joy is giving a singing lesson while her Burmese cat wails outside.

If I were to leave home without a watch?

A tiding of magpies picks through dirt tossing new slain grass.

Gill often used to read here on a bench by the Tumulus.

I never walk over Hampstead Heath without seeing the kestrel.

From behind the hedge a trumpet sounds an arpeggio suddenly.

Saturday morning outside the D'Aurio café drinking coffee.

A green woodpecker flies low out of the grass.

Under the awning of the bandstand a man performing Taiji slows time.

We pull back the ivy and pass between the wings of the pond.

Carpe diem Anne tells me.

HAMPSTEAD RESORT

Hampstead, is in every respect a watering-place – except
in there being no sea. However, it possesses all the necessary attributes:
a vast palatial hotel crenelated with towers and turrets built
by The Suburban Hotel Company Limited, renowned for its grottoes,
extensive tea gardens and smoking cabins for the well to do,

taprooms and bowling alleys for the working class, its terraces
overlooking the Vale of Health, the dammed river Fleet;
an esplanade for the fashionable; bath-chairs, sand and sandpits,
donkey rides and other fairground entertainment for visitors;
boating, until a regrettable drowning incident; boys sailing

miniature boats and fishing for tadpoles with crooked pins
in the (freshwater) ponds; tribes of healthy children with their nursemaids;
parties supplied by the hotel with hot water for tea from twopence
to fourpence per head; a fancy stationers' shop, with the proper supply
of dolls, novels and illustrated notepaper; a photographic pavilion

for 'this style' of portraits (a style which would effectually prevent any
sensible person from entering the place of execution); the flagstaff –
ready to dip its colours to steamers, which, of course, from the nature
of the case, can never appear in the offing; country walks and rides
for those residents, so exclusive – eligible houses that edge the water,

more humble apartments without a view, to be let furnished; an old
church and a new church, chapel of ease, graveyard and benches of rest;
a chalybeate spring to restore the health; in fact, it has all
that can make the heart glad and place Hampstead on the list
of seabathing places – with the trifling omission mentioned above.

A CULTURE IS NO BETTER THAN ITS WOODS

When Constable painted this view, clear to the South Downs,
    the dome of St Paul's stood out clear

on the sky-line. Today, its outline disappears into the Shard,
    acute angles of glass piercing the clouds;

penthouses start at thirty million pounds, affording a view
    of Ascot and ships on the North Sea.

At the edge of the woods, Caen Wood, revenant of the great
    Atlantic forest, when red squirrels could cross

from the Severn to the Wash without touching the ground,
    home to outlaws and wild animals now extinct,

close to Athlone House and new apartment blocks, ugly
    inheritors of modernism, a man has built a hut:

Harry Hallowes, resident so long that the Land Registry had
    to grant him deeds of ownership, for his life-time.

THE WHITE HOUSE NEXT DOOR

They have spent a quarter of a million pounds
on marble tiles for the patio.

A cockatoo in a six-foot cubic cage has moved in
on its own: her neighbour opposite,

through binoculars, saw it arrive; someone
comes twice a day to feed it.

The underground swimming pool they excavated
has destroyed her foundations.

She can't go to the law. Their sharp lawyers
would take her to the cleaners.

VALE OF HEALTH

A misnomer: the Vale of Health was never
a refuge from the plague but an unhealthy
malarial swamp, originally called Hatch's Bottom
where Samuel Hatch made harnesses for horses.

Leigh Hunt lived here in a picturesque cottage,
visited by Keats, Shelley, Hazlitt and Byron,
who left these words from Cowper on the window –

> *Oh for a lodge in some vast wilderness,*
> *Some boundless contiguity of shade,*
> *Where rumour of oppression and deceit,*
> *Of unsuccessful or successful war,*
> *Might never reach me more.*

Behind tall townhouses with immaculate
lawns extending to the pond, the cottages remain
bearing blue plaques to more recent writers
including D.H. Lawrence and Rabindranath Tagore.

The Hampstead Heath Hotel long demolished
and replaced with a tavern and artists' studios,
where Stanley Spencer painted the heath *Helter
Skelter* and completed his *Cookham Resurrection*;

where William Coldstream painted in the 1930s.
For a few weeks I stood in for his model, asked
him questions about communism and Auden:
he told me he always tried to paint what he saw.

IN THE COPSE OF OLDEST OAK

In the copse of oldest oak
you will find one tree
split at its base,
a red door opening
into a circular room
smelling of wood
and mushrooms,
a cover of fine down
laid over moss for a bed,
acorn cups and a dinner
service of leaf plates,
walnut shell bowls,
small twisted tables
and chairs of greenwood,
stairs that lead up
to a high snow door
and down to the Burrows.
Look carefully and
you will see the tiny face
at once joyful and sad
like a clown, of one
who takes a week
to eat a blackberry, bakes
his own chestnut bread
and brews mead,
collects pollen and nectar
but likes hazelnuts best,
dresses in leaves and bark
dyed bright red, spins
thread from the fluff of
dandelions and bumble bees,
rides on squirrels, flies
with migrating geese
and sleeps in a horse's ear;
as ancient as his tree, this is
one who remembers
everything and forgets
everything, whose
peaceful heart loves all
creatures of the wood.

CONSIDER THE BIRDS

A precise flocking, anisotropic,
each bird checking position
in relation to seven others
a wing-span apart,

a box, reel, swoop, frenzy of swifts
in their hundreds,
narrow wings scissoring the air,
shearing past our ears,
flying low over the field

as one
spinning gyroscope,

and we're flung
in a mimetic
centripetal swing,
the weak force of attraction,
loosening gravity,

a shift of centre in our cosmos
to a life on the wing,
a life of love on the wing,
feeding on the wing,
skimming the surface of the pond
taking sips of water,
bathing in falling rain,
coming to earth only to nest,

and ascend fast,
dark specks in the sky
high over the Lombardy poplar, far
above the city
on migration to the Sahara:

I run around you
my arms cast wide –

View from Hampstead Heath looking towards Harrow.
August 1821 5 p.m. very fine bright & wind after rain slightly
in the morning.

Study of clouds at Hampstead. 11th Sept. 1821. RA. 10 to 11.
Morning under the sun – Clouds silvery grey, on warm ground Sultry.
Light wind to the SW fine all day – but rain in the night following.

Hampstead Heath, Sun Setting over Harrow. 12th Sept. 1821.
... while making this sketch I observed the Moon rising very beautifully ...
due east over the heavy clouds from which the late showers had fallen.
Wind Gentle ... increasing from the North West.

The Road to the Spaniards, Hampstead, July 1822 looking NE 3pm
[previous to] a thunder squall wind N West.

Cloud Study. August, 27th. 1822 at 11 a.m. ... o'clock noon
looking Eastward large silvery clouds ... wind Gentle at S West.

London from Hampstead with a Double Rainbow, 1831, between 6
and 7 o clock Evenings June.

This, the first diagram of a double rainbow, shows
        the precise angles of primary and secondary bow,

its spectrum inverted, noting that the height depends
        upon time of day and year

and that a rainbow cannot be seen obliquely
        as a viewer must always keep the sun

over the shoulder: *a mild arch of promise ...*
        Flashing brief splendour through the clouds awhile.

WELL WALK

No water now flows from the fountain
on Well Walk,
where Stuarts and Georgians came to Hampstead's
serene air
to take the cure for shingles, scrofula,
diseases of skin and eye,
and after the bitter taste of chalybeate water
danced and gambled,
listened to Purcell and the latest songs.

Here, where Keats lived at Number 1
during his long struggle
writing *Endymion*,
and Constable lived at Number 6 with his wife,
then alone with his seven children,
on the site of the old Pump Room
Katharina Wolpe plays her father's music
'schrecklich, schrecklich laut'
with arm or fist –
Stehende Musik, 1925,
music of stasis,
known for its lack of development
except between two movements loud and rapid
as gun-fire
there is an interval of such ease,
a sweet melody
blossoming.

ZENITH

Hot sun pours into my head
where a *horn* may have grown,
a spear of keratin hard
as nails, hooves of cows,
feathers, beaks and claws
of the *crow, corvus, cornix*;
a curved horn, *curvus*,
shaped like a *kernel* of *corn*,
growing *cresco, grandis*, grass
from my *crown, corona*,
like a stalk, uncurling
into leaf as music. How we
may have passed, our feet bare,
through the Baal fires of Beltane,
running with our cattle,
sons and daughters. Leaves
of chestnut already brown, dry
and crackling in the sun, fireweed
gone over, desiccated to white
and blown to seed;
canopy expanding and heaving
into the sky, the city gleaming
with satisfaction
in that late stroke of light
before everything changes. Then
I will lose those adamantine
doubts via the suture
of my skull, through which I
          will leave this world.

5

…To where the Fleet-ditch, with disemboguing streams
Rolls the large tribute of dead dogs to Thames,
The King of Dykes!
Alexander Pope

AGAIN THE FALL

Again the rain will fall,
geese depart,
city streets darken;

the blast of autumn sun flare
against the city towers
as though on fire.

Again the fall of fine ash.
Again the fall of will.

Look further into the grain of things.
Listen to the silence.

THE ORDER OF THINGS

Why must we see one thing
in terms of another
more familiar –
someone, somewhere,
we already know?
pacifying the raucous mind
with mimesis,
and looking not
for the singular light
of revelation
that will disrupt
the line of history.

Antithesis of questioning –
our symmetry, hands
and feet radial from one trunk,
feeling and thought splayed
like an array
of rowan leaves,
granting reassurance
until the wind turns
us towards doubt,
our skin thins
and everything
becomes tangible.

WHAT DO WE WANT?

It's an ancient cry
like a hunting horn,
this voice of the demo,

vox populi
of the 99%,
St Paul's demarcated

from the Square Mile;
Ceci n'est pas le capitalisme
written on hazard tape.

It's the fall we want –
the fall of inequity,
to shut down what Keynes

called the *casino,*
the market's roulette
playing dice with our lives.

A GRAND DEMOCRACY OF FOREST TREES

instead of being a wide heath of Furse and Briars,
with here and there a remote Oak or Pine…

a grand democracy of Forest Trees –
this was Keats's vision for humanity:

our inner citadels open to each other
like flowers opening their leaves,

passive and receptive; without dispute
or assertion but whispering, the way

he would have whispered in Fanny's ear,
as they walked across the Heath

and surely rested here at Bird Bridge,
its iron-rich stream a deep rust, where

we sit now observing the nuthatch
and treecreeper spiral the birch,

a rat hurry over the bank where Keats,
the apothecary, would have searched

for coltsfoot, bogbean, sphagnum moss,
lungwort, wanting to do some good.

LONDON'S BURNING

London's burning, London's burning.
Fetch the engine, fetch the engine.
Fire, fire! Fire, fire!
Pour on water, pour on water.

Pudding Lane towards Old Bailey.
Fires roaring, flames are soaring.
Ring ring! Ring ring!
Wake the women, wake the children.

Newgate prison gates are open.
Take to water, skiffs and lighters.
Run, run! Run, run!
Save the houses, save the horses.

Roofs collapsing, buildings tumbling,
dry as tinder, falling timber.
Help him! Help her!
Hear the crackling, smell the charring.

Thomas Farryner, King Charles' baker,
baking pigeons, baking corpses.
Duke of York! King's guard!
Blow up houses, clear a barrier.

Fountains boiling, stone walls whitening,
molten lead and melting iron.
Hell's bells! Hell's bells!
Guildhall's glowing, burn the gallows.

St Paul's burning, St Paul's yearning,
find a scapegoat, find a fall guy.
Confess! Say yes!
Hang at Tyburn, swing at Tyburn.

Ask God's pardon, pray for sinners –
turn the great wind, turn the east wind.
Due south! Due south!
Douse the fire in the river.

Fetter Lane by Mitre Tavern
stands a great tree, bounds the City.
New world! New world!
Build new London from the ruins.

TUMULUS

Neither the site of Boudicca's grave
nor a Bronze Age barrow;

not even, as once thought, a pre-Roman
burial ground but a rubbish tip

of Delft pottery, seeded with Scots pine,
ringed by iron railings and benches

facing the sun. Under this bench
a deep hole: a small tree keeled over?

bush grubbed out? a burrow
for rabbit, fox or other small mammal?

I find myself on my knees, digging,
frantic as the dispossessed.

GODSPELL

Godspell,
a corruption of the Old English
for good news:

with the fall of the word
from the world
how many names are there for irony?

It's said that words do not break bones
but words can break and
mend the heart.

I stepped down from the dead oak
and simply walked away,
my hands on fire.

TWICE BORN

As though I were asked to polish
each blade of grass
and this time, to not question
the meaning of the task
and to not fail,
               I would follow you,

the way a pair of wrynecks,
old world woodpeckers, stepping carefully
along a horizontal bough,
turn their heads
through 180°
to look back at us,

and I would renounce everything,
for you are midwife
and funeral bearer:
               Hope, the name
I believe you were given,
for hope can come from such extremes.

FOR THE OAK

Heartfelt
flight of heart

wild at heart
heart willed

heart worn
heart of iron

in good heart
heart of the dog

heartache
take my heart

heart of cherry
heart of cheer

learn by heart
kernel of the heart

heartland
lend us heart

lose heart
heartless

heartleaf
heart of life

stolen heart
heart of steel

in bad heart
heart of the bud

faint of heart
find the heart

light hearted
heart of the lute

heartsease
easy in heart

heartstrings
strong of heart

heartwood
wooden heart

broken heart
heart of the brook

heavy heart
heart of heaven

oracular heart
heart of oak.

BUBO BUBO

Imagine when Eurasian eagle owls,
the largest owls in the world,

flew free over Hampstead Heath.
I've only ever seen them in a cage

at Golders Hill zoo; one always asleep,
the other to the fore, wide awake.

Only when the dusk starts to fall does the owl
of Minerva spread its wings and fly –

how we understand history in Hegel's
view, with the hindsight of a new age;

the owl seeking its prey on the wing
swerves into the dark unknown.

WYLDE'S FARMHOUSE

It's still here, Old Wylde's farmhouse,
remarkably unchanged since the time Blake
used to stay with Linnell and his family
during his late years, when he worked
on engravings for *The Divine Comedy*;
walking from Lambeth through the city
to this wood he called 'the Dante Wood',
often leaving late at night in darkness,

no moon, no shadows, no distinction,
only in my mind, pitiless fear; one of his
last images, *God creating the universe*, a man
with a pair of compasses, measuring,
dividing the absolute into infinity and
finitude, and therefore creating space.

VETERAN

Veteran,
survivor of famine,
plague, flood, fire and pestilence;

survivor of the Gulf wars, World Wars, Boer, Crimean, Civil Wars,
Wars of the Roses, Crusades –

common oak, English oak,
branches square to the trunk, flailing
in the wind, sinews twisting,
accumulating angular momentum
in its heart,
distributing stress
over its breadth
like a broad back,
strengthening the wood,

crooked wood, compass wood
for building hulls;
masts from the straight boles of sessile oak,
durmast oak;
forests felled for Elizabethan ships.

Now, in old age, feral,
bark expanding, fissured, calloused,
slipping to the underside
of its bough,

this hollow oak stands
stag-headed
crimson,
roots hefted to the surface,
its lower branches

a violent green persistence.

Sinking through the lock
at Limehouse,
the last wooden sailing barge, *Cabby*,
built in 1928, spills
out into the Thames basin,

cold light of a winter dawn
ricochets off the city towers of Canary Wharf,
the FSA at Cabot Square,
a red light on the pyramid roof
of One Canada Square.

We are sailing east
passing those grey blocked remains of factories,
heaps of cement and gravel,
graves of docks,
crossing the zero prime meridian
at Greenwich,
back-end of a grand building, the Royal Observatory,
then the O2
dome of needles;

each twist and turn
of the river back-
dropped by the sky-line of modernity,
the panopticon following us
up the rise and flow
of tide,
brine brackish and pushing upriver against
the gainful engine, burning
diesel and urgent,

through the Thames Barrier raised
for the rush of North Sea,
strong arms of a sinuous current carrying
barges and container ships

into dock,
grain and aggregates,
crude oil and petroleum to storage depots,
sugar to the Tate & Lyle refinery at Silvertown.

The river opening its mouth,
swallowing
the waste
digested in sewage plants
at Beckton, Crossness, Longreach,
barges from the City
chugging
to the tall-stacked incinerators,

Thames becoming sea;
the city behind us shrinking
as we slip low under Queen Elizabeth Bridge,
Gravesend,
to the port of Tilbury,
where the Windrush docked in 1948,
P&O's London International Cruise Terminal
for those large white floating hotels
basking downriver

from Veolia's landfill site
at Rainham;
recycled metals, plastics, paper and card,
crushed, shredded, baled and sold,
methane mutated into electricity,
artificial hills of stinking waste in transition between tip
and green landscape
eased with turrets to vent the gas,
picked over by wheeling flocks of white herring gulls.

A single apple tree laden
with bright red fruit.
The Thames dredged for a wild bird reserve.

In the distance,
32 km away, yet clearly visible,
the red light blinking.

APPLE GATHERERS
by Stanley Spencer, 1912–1913

Painted over a first rendition
of *The Resurrection*;

a surplus of apples,
green symmetrical bramley,

russet and cox, occasionally split,
skins revealing juicy flesh.

And this is what I wish for you –
the din of happiness all around me everywhere,

after all the labour and care,
sweet fragrance of apple blossom

amidst pale curled leaves
and the harvest yet to come.

THE KEEPER OF TREES

Keeper of trees,

clipboard and pen in hand

is monitoring the great oaks,

checking for disease

and the consequences of age,

carefully examining the acorns –

bunches of green sessile,

so easily mistaken for grapes,

their ganglion nerves;

yellow acorns of common oak,

decorative as toys,

so festive they must be gifts,

turning glossy brown

like dark chocolate;

hairy cups of Turkey oak

that could be the wiry nests of miniature birds;

mossy cups of Lucombe

soft as down;

tight acorns of ilex bright green and neat,

mimicking petit pois;

flat acorns of red pin oak

squashed into shallow cups resembling berets;

here, where large cut-out leaves

translucent yellow, orange and red,

stream light

with the antique qualities

of wine goblets

or the stained glass of a cathedral

                into the deep wooded glade,

                          its scent reminding me

of that panelled room filled with instruments –

xylophone, glockenspiel, drums, tabla, bells, tambourine, gongs,

                                  triangle, maracas,

              two grand pianos facing
              each other;

              you, who listened to my broken notes,
                        leading me,
                        following me,

you, who played Rachmaninoff's
              Concerto no. 2 in C minor

              now, on the other side of the river.

NOTES

PREFACE
George Oppen, 'Part of the forest', *New Collected Poems* (New York: New Directions, 2002), ed. E. Weinberger.

1
PREFACE
W. G. Sebald, *Austerlitz* (London: Hamilton, 2001).

CONSTABLE'S VIEW
C. R. Leslie, *Memoirs of the Life of John Constable* (London: Phaidon, 1995).

THE VIEW FROM PARLIAMENT HILL
Karl Marx and Friedrich Engels, *The Manifesto of the Communist Party*, 1847, in *Marx/Engels Selected Works* (Moscow: Progress Publishers, 1969) vol. one, trans. Moore and Engels.

THE ART OF WAR
Leon Trotsky, *Literature and Revolution*, 1924 (New York: Russell & Russell, 1957).

2
PREFACE
Bertolt Brecht 'Motto to the "Svendborg Poems" (1938) in *Edwin Morgan Collected Translations* (Manchester: Carcanet, 1996).

GREENMANS
Gillian Tindall, *The Fields Beneath* (London: Eland Books, 2011).

SANDY HEATH
Illustrated London News, September 1871.

3
PREFACE
H. D. 'The Walls Do Not Fall', *Trilogy* (Manchester: Carcanet, 1997).

SPRING
Plotinus, *The Enneads* (London: Penguin, 1991) VI, 9, 1. trans. John Dillon and Stephen MacKenna. The concept of Personhood is drawn from the philosophy of C. S. Peirce.

CHORUS
Plotinus, *The Enneads* VI, 9, 9.

4
PREFACE
Philip Corner, *I Can Walk Through the World as Music (first walk)* (Barrytown, New York: Printed Editions, 1980).

HAMPSTEAD RESORT
Edward Walford 'Hampstead: Caen Wood and north end', *Old and new London: a narrative of its history, its people, and its places,* (London: Cassell, Petter and Gilpin, 1878).

'A CULTURE IS NO BETTER THAN ITS WOODS'
W.H. Auden 'Bucolics, II: Woods', for Nicolas Nabakov, *The Shield of Achilles* (London: Faber & Faber 1956).

CONSTABLE THE NUBILOUS SKYING
Constable's own notes made on his paintings and drawings.

WELL WALK
Stefan Wolpe, *Program Notes*, Stefan Wolpe Society http://www.wolpe.org/ Reference also to *Stationary Music*, 2005, a film by Jayne Parker featuring Katharina Wolpe.

ZENITH
Gerard Manley Hopkins 'Extracts from An Early Diary, *September 24th, 1863*'.

5

PREFACE

Alexander Pope, *The Dunciad in Four Books*, 1743 (New York: Pearson Education Ltd., 1999).

BUBO BUBO

G.W.F. Hegel, *Philosophy of Right*, 1820, preface. *Grundlinien der Philosophie des Rechts*: '...die Eule der Minerva beginnt erst mit der einbrechenden Dämmerung ihren Flug.'

A GRAND DEMOCRACY OF FOREST TREES

John Keats, letter to John Hamilton Reynolds, Hampstead, 19 February 1818.

APPLE GATHERERS

Stanley Spencer notebook c. 1948; Tate Archive 733.8.35.

THE KEEPER OF TREES

For Sandra Brown: to go 'forward in hope into the unknown'.

Acknowledgements and my thanks to the editors of the following journals for publishing earlier versions of these poems: *Poetry Review, Poetry Wales, Roundyhouse* and *Shearsman*. Many thanks also to the Hawthornden Castle Fellowship for a writing residency in 2009.

As ever, I am especially grateful to Mimi Khalvati for her generosity and wisdom. I would also like to thank John Haynes, Jane Duran, Jacqueline Gabbitas, Aviva Dautch and Mimi's Monday class for all their comments and support.